Back to Basics™

YEARS 3 & 4

MONEY AND PERCENTAGES

Ann Baker

Illustrated by Janice Bowles

About this book

Each unit in this book begins with a brief **explanation** of a concept or a strategy. You are encouraged to read this explanation with your child and, where appropriate, to use everyday materials and examples to give meaning to the concepts.

We practise is a worked example for you and your child to discuss together, paying particular attention to the thinking processes required to understand the concept or apply the strategy.

You practise gives your child the opportunity to practise the concept or strategy. It also indicates how well your child understands the new material and often includes problem-solving questions to ensure that your child has mastered the concept or strategy.

If further support is required, you and your child's teacher can devise a plan to ensure that all the basic concepts are fully understood and consolidated.

The **Tests** at the end of the book are provided to check that the concepts are fully understood. Test 1 can be done after Units 1–10 are completed and Test 2 when the book is finished.

Meet 'BOB' – Back Of the Book

At the end of each unit, BOB reminds your child to go to the Answers section at the back of the book.

Mathematical Content

This book has been designed to cover the concepts of money and percentages that your child will encounter in **Year 3** and **Year 4**. It also covers some concepts from **Year 5** and **Year 6**. The units provide a comprehensive coverage of the following Key Topics from the **Australian Curriculum: Mathematics**.

Australian Curriculum : Mathematics

YEAR 3

Represent money values in multiple ways and count the change required for simple transactions to the nearest five cents (ACMNA059)

YEAR 4

Solve problems involving purchases and the calculation of change to the nearest five cents with and without digital technologies (ACMNA080)

YEAR 5

Create simple financial plans (ACMNA106)

YEAR 6

Investigate and calculate percentage discounts of 10%, 25% and 50% on sale items, with and without digital technologies (ACMNA132)

Contents & Checklist

Unit	Page		completed
	4	How to use this book	
1	6	Counting silver coins	☐
2	8	Mixed coin counting	☐
3	10	Dollars and cents	☐
4	12	Adding money amounts	☐
5	14	Giving change	☐
6	16	Rounding up and down	☐
7	18	Rounding shopping bills	☐
8	20	Multiplying money amounts	☐
9	22	How much?	☐
10	24	Problem solving with money	
11	26	A picnic budget	☐
12	28	Percentages	☐
13	30	10% and more	☐
14	32	Shopping receipts and GST	☐
15	34	50%, 25% and 20%	☐
16	36	On special	☐
17	38	Making a budget	☐
18	40	Calculator percentages	☐
19	42	Foreign currencies	☐
20	44	Problem solving	☐
	46	Test 1 & 2	☐
	48	Answers	

Writing and Talking about MONEY and PERCENTAGES

Australian currency

Denomination is the value of a coin or a note. In Australia, the coin denominations are 5c, 10c, 20c, 50c, $1 and $2, and the note denominations are $5, $10, $20, $50 and $100. Other countries have different denominations, such as pounds and pence in the United Kingdom.

Getting change

When you buy something and you give more money than the goods actually cost, you get change, which is usually given in the least number of coins and/or notes. To make sure you have the correct change, you can **count up** from the starting price using the coin denominations. Look at the number line below – it shows the counting sequence for the change from $5 for an item that cost $3.25.

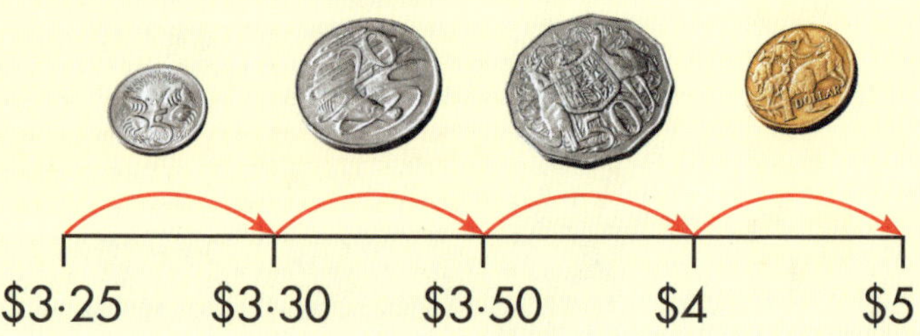

$3·25 $3·30 $3·50 $4 $5

Rounding and estimating

Rounding and estimating money amounts is really useful when you are shopping.

If you round to the nearest dollar amount you will have a good idea of how much your shopping should cost.

Goods and Services Tax

In Australia, a 10% tax is paid on most goods and services (GST). 10% is easy to work out. For example, 10% of $10 is $1 and 10% of $100 is $10. Remembering this will help you work out the GST on other amounts.

Percentage discounts

When there is a sale or a product is on special, the saving is often shown as a percentage discount, which tells you how much you will save in every dollar. For example, a 20% discount means that you will save 20c in every dollar. So if you spend $15 then you will save $3, which means the item will cost $12.

GAME CARD IDEAS

Cut out the game cards – they will last longer if they are laminated. Here are some games for you to try.

$250 or Broke

A game for two players.

Each player starts with 10 points and is dealt three picture shopping cards. The aim is to spend as close to $250 as possible, without overspending.

Players take turns to either take a card from the deck and add it to their collection, or say "finish" if they have reached $250 or close, and then wait for their opponent to finish. If a player goes over $250, then they lose a point.

If neither goes over, then the player with the lower value loses a point.

Play continues until one player loses all their points.

$50 LIMIT

Similar to $250 *or Broke*, but both players are dealt two picture shopping cards each and the aim is to spend as close to $50 as possible at the end of each round.

Players then take turns to either take a card from the deck and add it to their collection, or choose to discard a card. To be successful, continuous estimating is required and decisions made on those estimates are important.

Greatest Saver

A game for 2–4 players. Create two piles of cards – one for the shopping cards and another for the percentage cards.

Players take two cards, one from each pile. Each player then works out the savings that can be made on their shopping card using their percentage card. The player with the greatest saving wins the round and gets to keep their pair of cards. The other players must discard their cards onto a discard pile. Play continues in this way until all of the cards have been used. The player with the most pairs wins.

This can be made more challenging by using two shopping cards and one percentage card. Players add the two shopping cards and work out the percentage. It can be fun to play this game until one player has saved $100 dollars or more.

For the first few times you play these games, it is recommended that you use pencil and paper and/or a calculator to help your child to work out the answers.

NOTE: Games are meant to be fun and provide practice without stress. It is recommended that you stop playing while you are still having fun and then your child will want to play again another time.

COUNTING SILVER COINS

To be able to count silver coins you need to be good at speed counting in 5s, 10s, 20s and 50s. This is because silver coins come in 5c, 10c, 20c and 50c (cents). Try speed counting in 5s to find the value of these 5c coins.

Did you count twenty 5c coins? The total value of the coins is 100c or $1.

Speed count in 20s to work out the value of these 20c coins.

Did you count five 20c coins? This makes $1.

A fast way to count these 10c coins is by **grouping them in 10s**. Then you count on from $1 to $1.10, then $1.20.

How much are six 5c coins worth? Show the counting sequence and the total value.

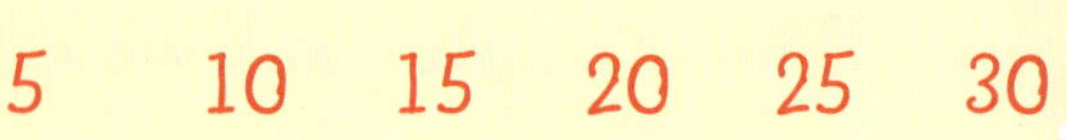

Total value = 30c

We practise

I have four coins in my hand that have a total value of 80c. What coins are they?

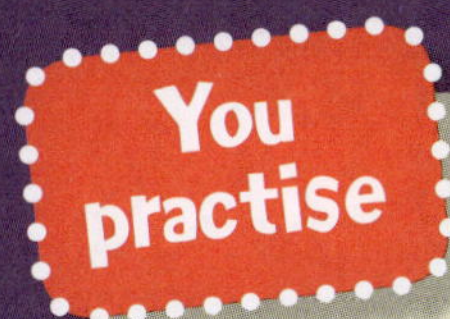

Show the counting sequence and the total value for these coins.

____ ____ ____ ____ ____ ____ ____ = _______ c

__ __ __ __ __ __ __ __ __ __ = _______ c

____ ____ ____ ____ ____ = _______ c or $ _______

____ ____ ____ = _______ c or $ _______

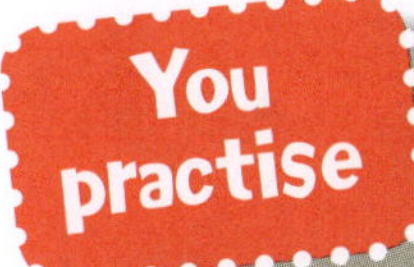

Draw the coins that are needed to make these amounts.

35c in 5c coins

60c in 10c coins

80c in 20c coins

$2.50 in 50c coins

MIXED COIN COUNTING

Banks and shops sort coins into their **denomination**, for example, grouping all the 5c coins together and all the 10c coins together, so that they can **speed count** the coins at the end of the day.

You can count coins in any order, but it saves brain time to work smart.

Look at this collection of silver coins.

The quickest way to work out their value is to rearrange them into a **different sequence**.

Start with the **50c** coin and then the **10c** coin, which makes 60c. Then add the **20c** to make 80c, then add the two **5c** coins (10c). The total value is **90c**.

Try counting the coins in different sequences to see which works best for you.

We practise

Show a speed counting sequence for this set of coins.

50 60 70 75 80 = 80c

What is the total value of these coins? Circle the correct amount.

25c 55c 75c

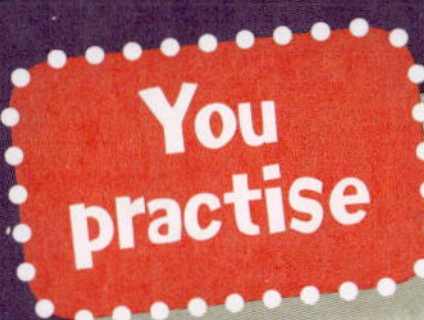

Show a speed counting sequence for each set of coins.

____ ____ ____ ____ ____ = ____ c

Remember to use the quickest way!

____ ____ ____ ____ ____ = ____ c

____ ____ ____ ____ ____ ____ ____ = ____ c or $ ____

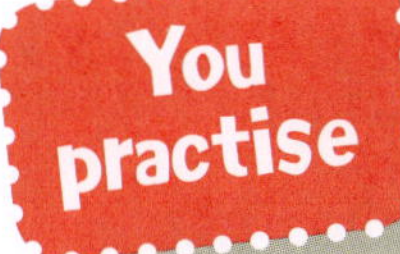

What is the total value of each set of coins? Circle the correct amount.

    = 25c 30c 40c

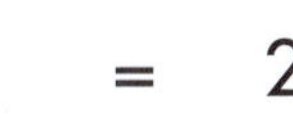

    = 75c 60c 55c

           = 85c 95c $1.05

BOB time!

UNIT 3

DOLLARS AND CENTS

You know that 5c, 10c, 20c and 50c are **silver coins** and $1 and $2 are **gold coins**.

You also know that 100c equals $1, so let's look at how to **count combinations of all these coins.**
Look at this collection of coins.

To find out what these coins are worth altogether, find all the gold coins first – this tells you how many dollars there are ($5). Then sort and count the silver coins to find out how many cents there are altogether (35c). Then add the two together to find that total value ($5.35).

When you pay for something, it's best to have the correct amount of money using the **least number of coins and notes.** This also applies to when you give or receive change.

The coins below show how to pay $2.75 using the least number of coins.

We practise

Write the value of the dollars and cents and then the total.

$*3*
*85*c
Total $*3.85*

Show how to make $3.35 using the least number of coins.

$2 $1
20c 10c 5c

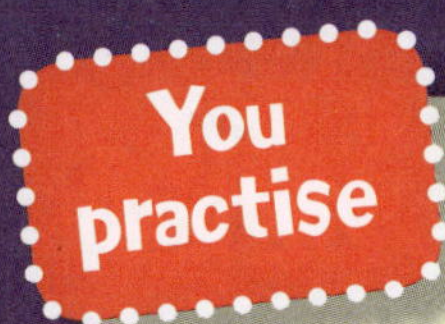

How much is each set of coins worth altogether? Write the value of the dollars and cents and then the total.

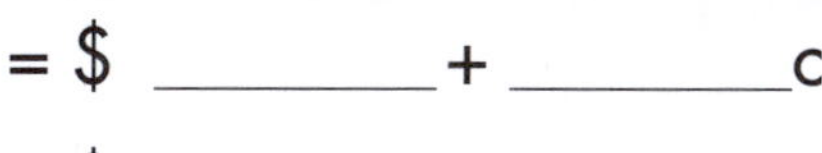

= $ ________ + ________c

= $ ________

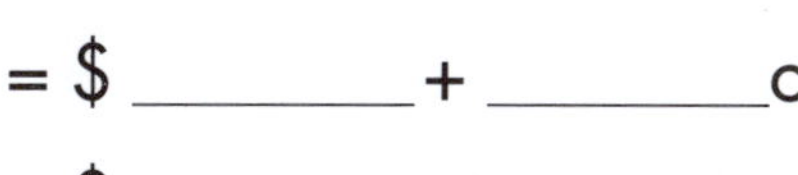

= $ ________ + ________c

= $ ________

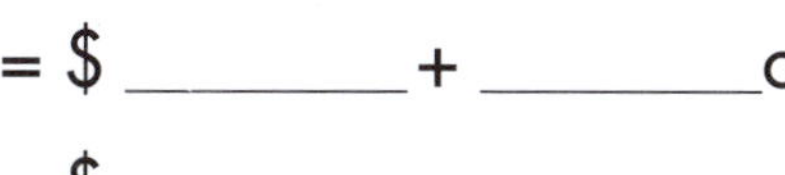

= $ ________ + ________c

= $ ________

= $ ________ + ________c

= $ ________

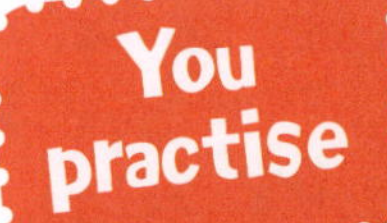

Show how to make each amount using the least number of coins.

$2.60

$3.55

$5.85

$3.95

BOB time!

UNIT 4

ADDING MONEY AMOUNTS

When you go shopping, you don't usually use paper and a pencil to work out how much two or more items will cost. However, there are strategies that can help you work out how much you will spend.

One strategy is to **split amounts to match the coins** that you have. Here is an example.

Buy two erasers at 65c each

65c is made with

put it altogether

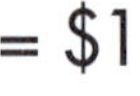
= $1

= 20c

= 10c

$1.30

With a little practice you will be able to do this in your head without looking at the coins. Try it and see.

I know that two 50c coins make $1. I can use this to help me to work out if I have enough money to buy **two** things that cost 65c each.

We practise

Show how to work out how much two apples at $1.60 each will cost.

Buy $1.60 $1.60

Cost
$1 + $1 = $2
50c + 50c = 100c
10c + 10c = 20c
$3.20

Show how to work out how much one apple at $1.60 and one banana at $1.50 will cost.

Buy $1.60 $1.50

Cost
$1 + $1 = $2
50c + 50c = 100c
10c = 10c
$3.10

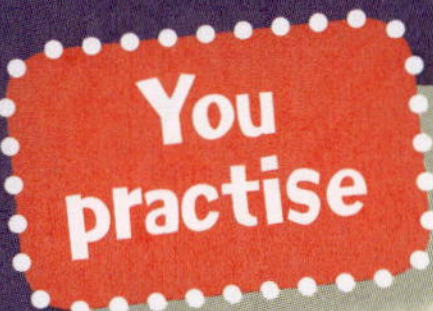

Show how to work out how much these items will cost.

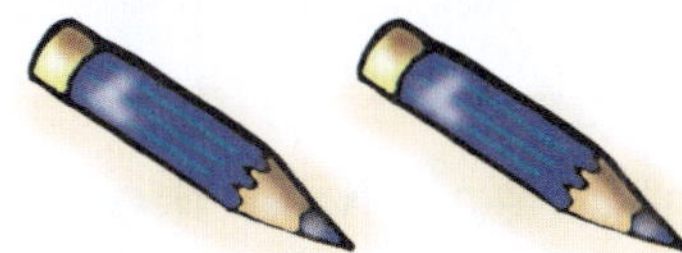

$1.55 each

Total

$ ________

Remember to think in terms of coins.

$1.35 each

Total

$ ________

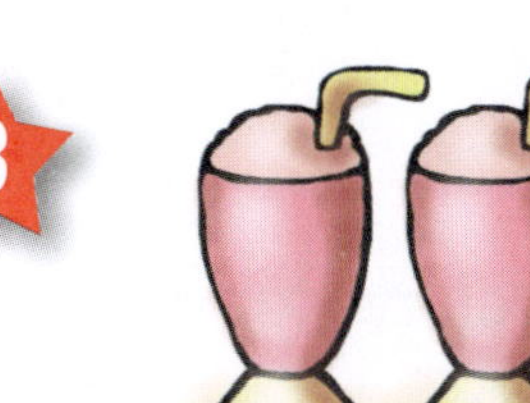

$1.20 each

Total

$ ________

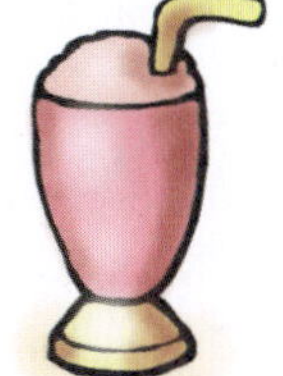

$2.25 $1.20

Total

$ ________

$1.55 $1.55 $1.35

Total

$ ________

$2.25 $1.35

Total

$ ________

BOB time!

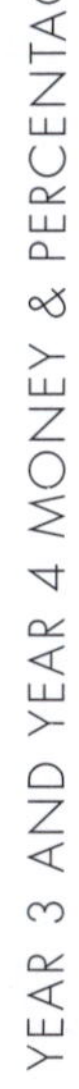

UNIT 5

GIVING CHANGE

When you pay for something and are given change, it is important to check that you have been given the correct amount using the least number of coins.

There is an easy way to do this.

For example, when you buy an apple for $1.65 and pay with a $2 coin, this is the change you should receive.

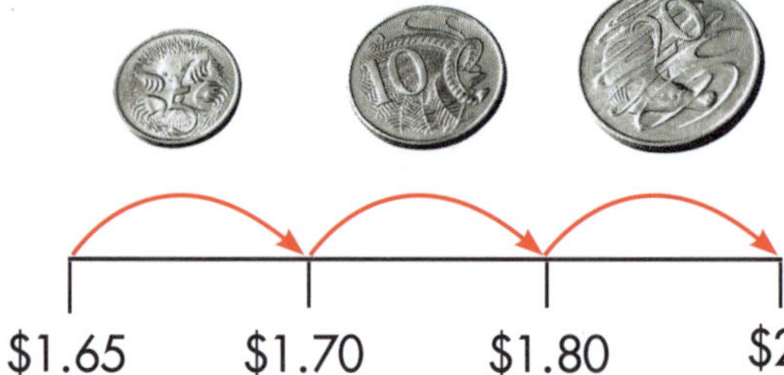

Add the coins to check that it is the correct change (35c).

I always want my change in the least number of coins or my purse gets too heavy.

Here is an example of change that has notes as well as coins.

Buy for $135.50 Pay with $150

Change = $14.50

What is the correct change with the least number of coins? Use the number line to show your answer.

Buy a cake $1.25  Pay with $2 

We practise

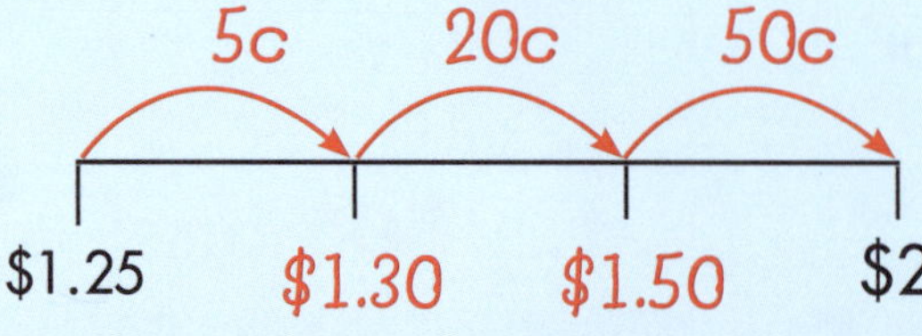

Change = 75c

You practise What is the correct change with the least number of coins? Use the number line to show your answer.

Buy a muffin $1.35 Pay with $2 

$1.35 ———— $2

Change = ________

Buy a burger $2.25 Pay with $4  

$2.25 ———— $4

Change = ________

Buy a pumpkin $3.50 Pay with $5 

$3.50 ———— $5

Change = ________

Buy a magazine $2.70 Pay with $10 

$2.70 ———— $10

Change = ________

Buy a book $27.50 Pay with $40 

$27.50 ———— $40

Change = ________

UNIT 6

ROUNDING UP AND DOWN

If you are buying something that costs $1.99 or $19.98, then it is impossible to pay with the correct money. This means that you have to round up or down to the nearest 5c.

If an item costs $1.78, it rounds up to $1.80, but if it is $1.77, it rounds down to $1.75. The number line below shows why this is so.

$1.70 $1.71 $1.72 $1.73 $1.74 **$1.75** $1.76 $1.77 $1.78 $1.79 **$1.80**

Notice that all the amounts between $1.70 and $1.80 are marked. The **start** and **finish** amount are in red and so is the midpoint $1.75.

To find out the **nearest 5** to any number, all you need to do is **count the jumps**. It is only 2 jumps on from $1.78 to $1.80, but it is 3 jumps back to $1.75.

That means that $1.78 is closer to $1.80 than it is to $1.75, which is why it is rounded up.

$1.72 is only two jumps from $1.70, so it rounds down.

Use the number line to show how to round $1.27 to the nearest 5c.

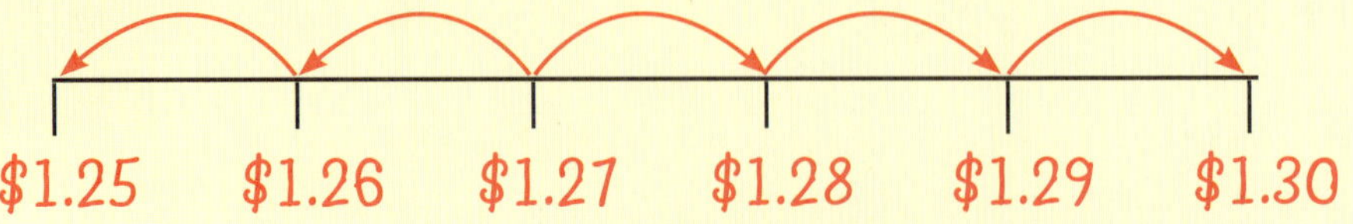

$1.25 $1.26 $1.27 $1.28 $1.29 $1.30

$1.27 rounds down to $1.25

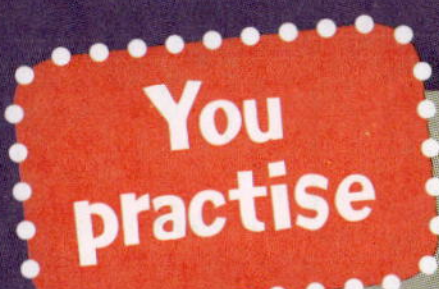

Round each amount up or down to the nearest 5c.
Hint: the answers are in the grid below.

1. $2.01 rounds ________ to $ ________ ☐

2. $1.52 rounds ________ to $ ________ ☐

3. $2.32 rounds ________ to $ ________ ☐

Don't forget to write whether you round up or down.

4. $8.98 rounds ________ to $ ________ ☐

5. $2.36 rounds ________ to $ ________ ☐

6. $7.02 rounds ________ to $ ________ ☐

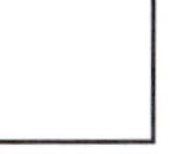

7. $5.56 rounds ________ to $ ________ ☐

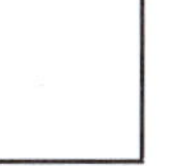

8. $3.38 rounds ________ to $ ________ ☐

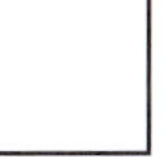

9. $6.56 rounds ________ to $ ________ ☐

10. $1.68 rounds ________ to $ ________ ☐

Write the letter that matches the correct answer to find a hidden message.

L	D	U	O	Y	E	W	D	I	L
$1.70	$9	$2.30	$1.50	$2	$3.40	$5.55	$7	$2.35	$6.55

BOB time!

ROUNDING SHOPPING BILLS

If you round down more than you round up, expect your estimate to be lower than the actual total.

It is useful when shopping to round amounts up or down to the nearest dollar or 50c to find an estimated total.

Would you have enough money to buy all of these items if you had only $10?

$1.90

$3.90

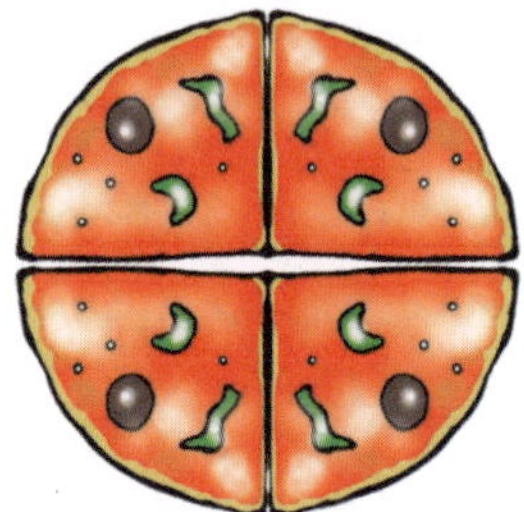

$4.55

The answer is no. An easy and fast way to work this out is to round each amount up or down to the nearest dollar or 50c.

$1.90 **rounds up** to $2

$3.90 **rounds up** to $4

$4.55 **rounds down** to $4.50

So then all you need to do is add $2 + $4 + $4.50 = $10.50 to see that $10 will not cover all three items.

We practise

Round each of these amounts to the nearest dollar. What is the estimated (not exact) total amount to the nearest dollar?

$1.75 rounds up to $2

$3.15 rounds down to $3

Estimated amount $5

Round each of these amounts to the nearest dollar or 50 cents and give the estimated total amount. Then find the actual amount with a calculator.

Amount	Rounds to
$3.95	$4
$2.55	$2.50
$6.45	$6.50
Actual $12.95	Estimated $13

You practise Round each amount up or down to the nearest dollar. What is the estimated total amount?

1

$2.20 rounds ________ to $ ________

$2.95 rounds ________ to $ ________ Estimated amount $ ________

2

$3.85 rounds ________ to $ ________

$3.90 rounds ________ to $ ________ Estimated amount $ ________

3

$6.80 rounds ________ to $ ________

$4.25 rounds ________ to $ ________ Estimated amount $ ________

Round each amount up or down to the nearest 50c or dollar. What is the estimated total amount? What is the actual amount?

4

$1.35 $ ________

$7.45 $ ________

Estimated $ ________ Actual $ ________

5

$2.75 $ ________

$3.75 $ ________

$3.99 $ ________

Estimated $ ________ Actual $ ________

Use your calculator to find the actual amounts.

6

$1.20 $ ________

$3.45 $ ________

$2.75 $ ________

Estimated $ ________ Actual $ ________

MULTIPLYING MONEY AMOUNTS

BARGAIN!

Four donuts only **$7.50**

Shops often have a special price if you buy more than one thing. Is this a bargain?

Here is one strategy for finding out.

Round $1.95 up to $2

4 × $2 = $8

But that is 5c more per donut than what they actually cost, which is 4 × 5c = 20c too much.

Adjust $8 – 20c = $7.80

So buying four donuts for $7.50 **saves 30c**.

I really only need to eat one donut, not four!

What if the donuts are **$1.75 each** or **four for $7**?

Is that a bargain?

A second strategy is to **split** the amount into manageable parts.

$1.75 = $1 + 50c + 25c

4 × $1 = $4   4 × 50c = $2   4 × 25c = $1

$4 + $2 + $1 = $7

The packet of four is not a bargain; it is exactly the same price.

We practise

Round and adjust to work out what three avocados at $1·45 each cost.

Round $1.45 up to $1.50

3 × $1.50 = $4.50

Adjust 3 × 5c = 15c

$4.50 + / − 15c = $4.35

Show how to split amounts for easy multiplying when you buy five oranges at 75c each.

75c = 50c + 25c

5 × 50c = $2.50

5 × 25c = $1.25

Total = $3.75

You practise Round and adjust to work out how much for the following items.

1 Four avocados at $1.45 each

Round: $1.45 _______ to $ _______

4 × $ _______ = $ _______ $ _______ +/− _______ c = $ _______

2 Three oranges at 95c each

Round: 95c _______ to $ _______

3 × $ _______ = $ _______ $ _______ +/− _______ c = $ _______

3 Six grapefruit at $1.90 each

Round: $1.90 _______ to $ _______

6 × $ _______ = $ _______ $ _______ +/− _______ c = $ _______

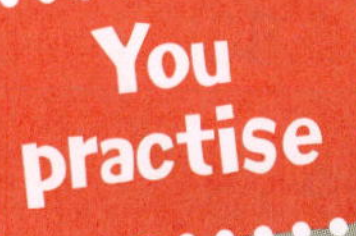

Show how to split amounts to find out how much for the following items.

4 Four hotdogs at $2.50 each

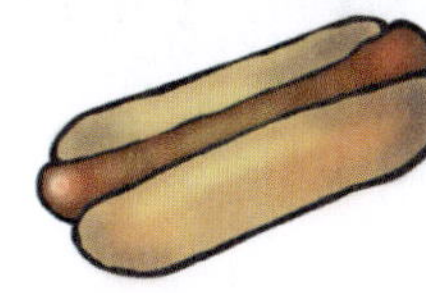

$2.50 = $ _______ + _______ c

4 × $ _______ = $ _______

4 × _______ c = $ _______ Total $ _______

5 Three burgers at $2.55 each

$2.55 = $ _______ + _______ c + _______ c

3 × $ _______ = $ _______

3 × _______ c = $ _______

3 × _______ c = _______ c Total $ _______

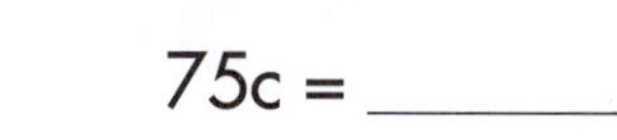

6 Five icy poles at 75c each

75c = _______ c + _______ c + _______ c

5 × _______ c = $_______

5 × _______ c = $_______

5 × _______ c = _______ c Total = $_______

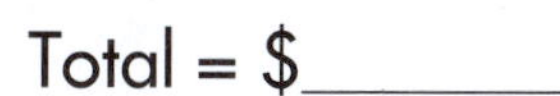

HOW MUCH?

A shopkeeper has made this poster to show his customers how much it costs to buy up to six items from his menu. He made the poster really quickly by rounding and splitting amounts.

Qty						
1	$1.25	$0.95	$1.75	$1.45	$3.25	$3.95
2	$2.50	$1.90	$3.50	$2.90	$6.50	$7.90
3	$3.75	$2.85	$5.25	$4.35	$9.75	$11.85
4	$5	$3.80	$7	$5.80	$13	$15.80
5	$6.25	$4.75	$8.75	$7.25	$16.25	$19.75
6	$7.50	$5.70	$10.50	$8.70	$19.50	$23.70

For six bananas think **6 × $1** and then **subtract 30 cents**. That's **$5.70**. This strategy saves brain space!

Which strategy would you use for 4 × $1.90?

Rounding 

Number splitting 

We practise

Complete this table, but remember to use smart strategies.

Qty	$1.25	$2.85
3	$3.75	$8.55
4	$5	$11.40

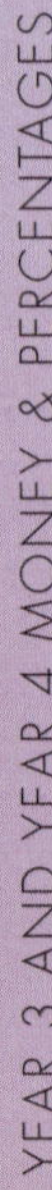

You practise

Complete this table. Shade the boxes red where you used rounding. Shade the boxes blue where you used splitting.

Remember, 4 × 25c = $1 and 75c + 25c = $1.

Qty					
1	$1.45	99c	$1.95	$3.75	$3.25
2					
3					
4					
5					
6					
7					
8					

BOB time!

PROBLEM SOLVING WITH MONEY

$1.55 $1.85 99c $2.35 $3.25

Clare bought an apple, a bottle of water and a muffin. She paid with a $10 note.

What change should Claire receive? What are the least number of coins for her change?

Notice how the important information is highlighted in blue and what has to be found out is highlighted in pink.

Before you start working on this problem, you need to **estimate** how much Clare has **spent** and how much **change** she should get. To do this, follow these steps:

Step 1 Round to find the estimated cost ($1.50 + $2 + $2.50 = $6)

Step 2 Estimate the change expected ($10 – $6 = $4)

Then use a calculator to work out the **exact amount** she has **spent**: $1.55 + $1.85 + $2.35 = $5.75

Use a number line to work out the **correct change** with the **least number of coins.**

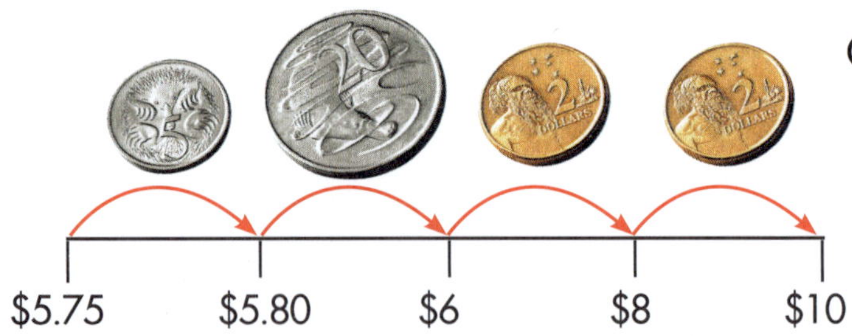

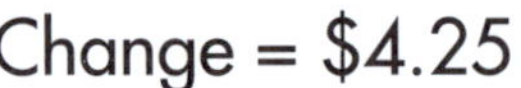

Change = $4.25

We practise

Highlight the important information and what has to be found out in this problem.

Jake has $6.50 and wants to buy a muffin ($2.35), a burger ($3.25) and an apple ($1.55). He makes an estimate and discovers that he needs more money.

What is his estimate? How much extra money does he need?

Estimate: $2.50 + $3 + $1.50 = $7

Exact amount: $2.35 + $3.25 + $1.55 = $7.15

Jake needs an extra $0.65 cents

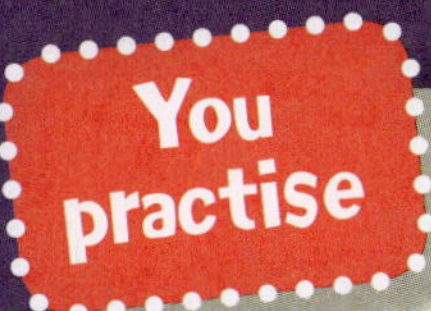

Highlight the important information and solve these problems. Use the prices listed on the opposite page.

1. Jake paid for an apple using a $1 coin and a 50c coin. What other coin did he use? ________

2. Clare used the exact money in the least amount of coins to pay for a muffin and a drink. Which coins did she use? ____________ ______________________________

3. The shopkeeper has an order for one of everything on the board. Estimate how much the order is worth. ______________________

Remember that you can use real coins and a calculator, but you must estimate first.

4. Mum bought Clare, Jake and herself each a bottle of water. How much did this cost? ________

5. Jake wants a muffin and a drink. Clare wants a burger and a drink. Jake estimates that the $10 note they have will cover it. Clare says it won't. Will $10 be enough? ________

6. Clare bought a muffin. Jake spent nearly $1 more than Clare. Which two items did Jake buy? ____________________________

7. Mum ordered 3 burgers and 3 bottles of water. How much did this cost? ________

8. Clare rounded the price of three items and the estimate was $6. What are the three items? ______________________________

9. How much change and what coins should the shopkeeper give Clare if she pays for an apple with a $10 note? ______________

10. How much do 6 bottles of water cost? ______________________

BOB time!

A PICNIC BUDGET

Clare and Jake have a $20 **budget** to buy food for a picnic for four people. Here are the items that they can select from.

Remember, it is important to round and make an estimate first.

This is Jake's plan and costing:

Buy	Estimate	Actual
2 apples at $1.85 each	$4	$3.70
1 orange juice at $5.45	$5.50	$5.45
1 choc milk at $3.95	$4	$3.95
2 subs at $2.45 each	$5	$4.90
Totals	**$18.50**	**$18**

We practise

Complete Clare's plan and costing. Remember to make the estimate before finding the actual total.

Buy	Estimate	Actual
2 packets chips at $2.15 each	$4	$4.30
3 subs at $2.45 each	$7.50	$7.35
1 muffin at $3.60	$4	$3.60
1 choc milk at $3.95	$4	$3.95
Totals	**$19.50**	**$19.20**
Total	$19	$19.20

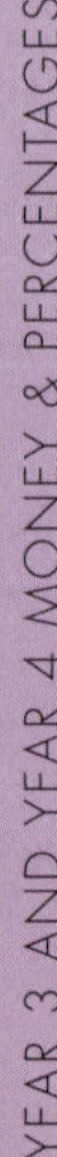

Back to Basics
MONEY & PERCENTAGES
YEARS 3 and 4

Back to Basics
MONEY & PERCENTAGES
YEARS 3 and 4

Back to Basics
MONEY & PERCENTAGES
YEARS 3 and 4

Back to Basics
MONEY & PERCENTAGES
YEARS 3 and 4

Back to Basics
MONEY & PERCENTAGES
YEARS 3 and 4

Back to Basics
FRACTIONS & DECIMALS
YEARS 3 and 4

Back to Basics
MONEY & PERCENTAGES
YEARS 3 and 4

Back to Basics
MONEY & PERCENTAGES
YEARS 3 and 4

Back to Basics
MONEY & PERCENTAGES
YEARS 3 and 4

Back to Basics
FRACTIONS & DECIMALS
YEARS 3 and 4

Back to Basics
MONEY & PERCENTAGES
YEARS 3 and 4

Back to Basics
MONEY & PERCENTAGES
YEARS 3 and 4

Back to Basics
MONEY & PERCENTAGES
YEARS 3 and 4

Back to Basics
FRACTIONS & DECIMALS
YEARS 3 and 4

Back to Basics
MONEY & PERCENTAGES
YEARS 3 and 4

Back to Basics
MONEY & PERCENTAGES
YEARS 3 and 4

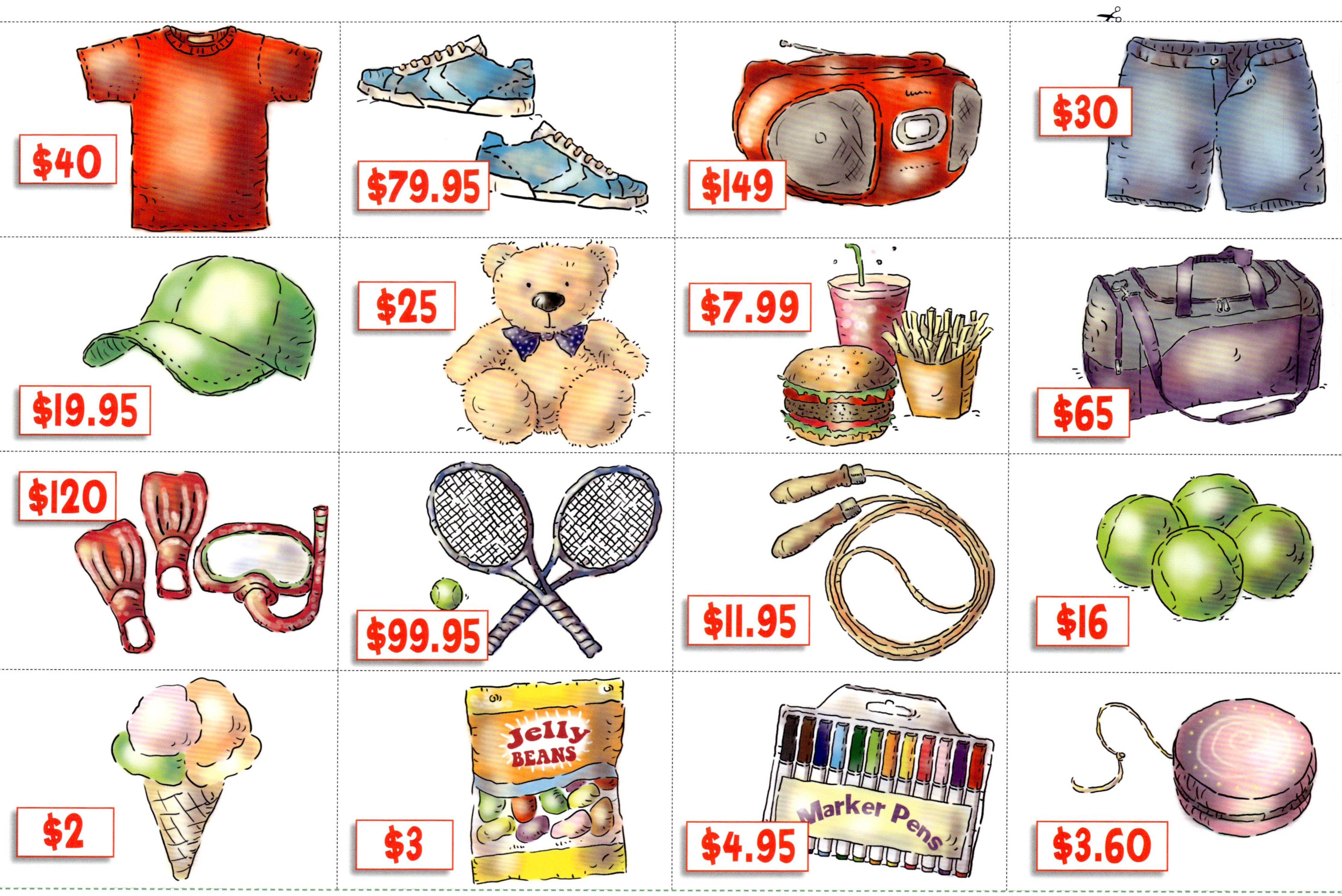
$40
$79.95
$149
$30
$19.95
$25
$7.99
$65
$120
$99.95
$11.95
$16
$2
$3
Jelly
BEANS
$4.95
Marker Pens
$3.60

Plus 10% GST	10% off	$\frac{1}{2}$ price	5% off
1% off	20% discount	25% off sale	Save 75%
11% price cut	21% off	Plus 10% GST	10% discount
5% saving	6% saving	50% off	25% discount

Back to Basics™

MONEY & PERCENTAGES

YEARS 3 and 4

Back to Basics™
MONEY & PERCENTAGES
YEARS 3 and 4

Back to Basics™
MONEY & PERCENTAGES
YEARS 3 and 4

Back to Basics™
MONEY & PERCENTAGES
YEARS 3 and 4

Back to Basics™
MONEY & PERCENTAGES
YEARS 3 and 4

Back to Basics™
MONEY & PERCENTAGES
YEARS 3 and 4

Back to Basics™
MONEY & PERCENTAGES
YEARS 3 and 4

Back to Basics™
MONEY & PERCENTAGES
YEARS 3 and 4

Back to Basics™
MONEY & PERCENTAGES
YEARS 3 and 4

Back to Basics™
MONEY & PERCENTAGES
YEARS 3 and 4

Back to Basics™
MONEY & PERCENTAGES
YEARS 3 and 4

Back to Basics™
MONEY & PERCENTAGES
YEARS 3 and 4

Back to Basics™
MONEY & PERCENTAGES
YEARS 3 and 4

Back to Basics™
MONEY & PERCENTAGES
YEARS 3 and 4

Back to Basics™
MONEY & PERCENTAGES
YEARS 3 and 4

Back to Basics™
MONEY & PERCENTAGES
YEARS 3 and 4

You practise

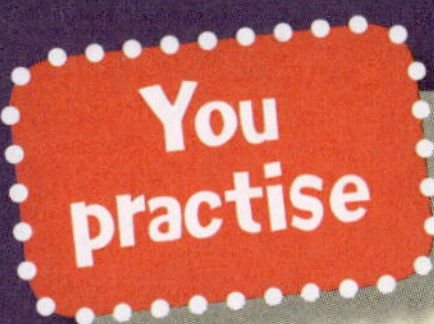

Use the items and prices opposite to do a picnic budget for six people with a budget of $35.

UNIT 11

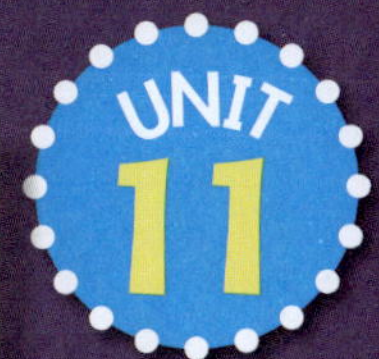

Remember that **rounding and number splitting can help** to work out actual costs.

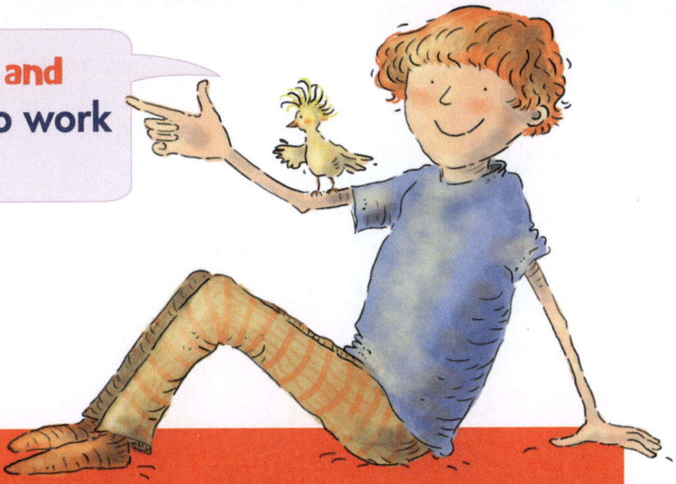

Buy	Estimate	Actual
Totals		

BOB time!

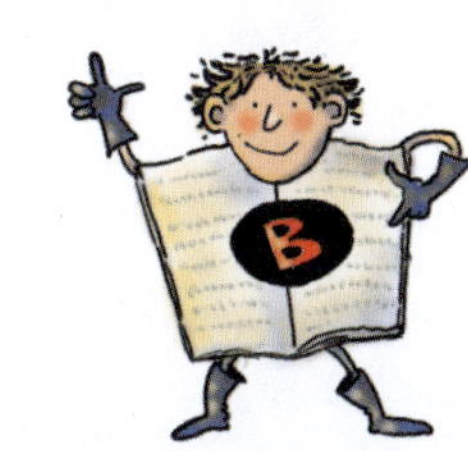

UNIT 12 PERCENTAGES

Per cent (%) means one part in a hundred.
For example, 1% is the same as $\frac{1}{100}$.

So what is a **percentage**? Any number that is used as a per cent is called a percentage.

Remember that 1% of 100 is 1. This fact will often come in handy.

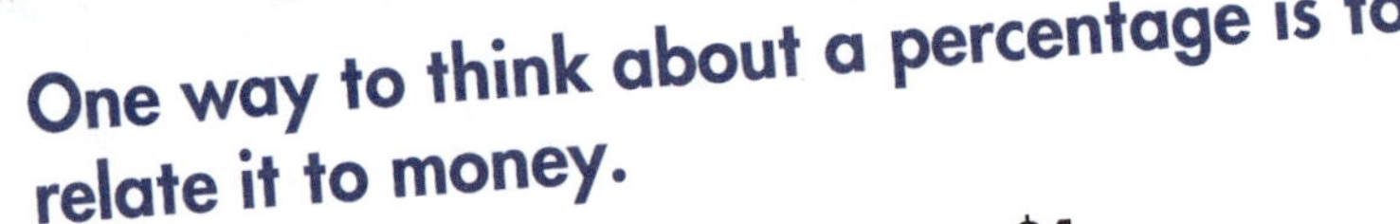

One way to think about a percentage is to relate it to money.

You know that there are 100c in \$1.

1% means 1 out of 100, so **1% of \$1 is 1c.**

You can use this fact to work with other amounts and percentages.

Use it to find 1% of \$6:

If 1% of \$1 = 1c

Then 1% of \$6 is 6 × 1c = 6c

And 8% of \$1:

If 1% of \$1 = 1c

Then 8% of \$1 is 8 × 1c = 8c

We practise

Show how to find 1% of \$7 using what you already know.

1% of \$1 = 1c

1% of \$7 = 7c

Show how to find 7% of \$10 using what you already know.

1% of \$1 = 1c

7% of \$1 = 7c

7% of \$10 = 70c

You practise Work out these percentage amounts.
Hint: the answers are in the grid below.

1. 4% of \$6 = ________ c

2. 1% of \$4 = ________ c

3. 5% of \$1= ________ c

4. 6% of \$1 = ________ c

5. 5% of \$5 = ________ c

6. 5% of \$2 = ________ c

7. 3% of \$1= ________ c

8. 5% of \$4 = ________ c

9. 6% of \$3 = ________ c

10. 3% of \$3 = ________ c

Remember to use what you know about 1% to work out these percentages.

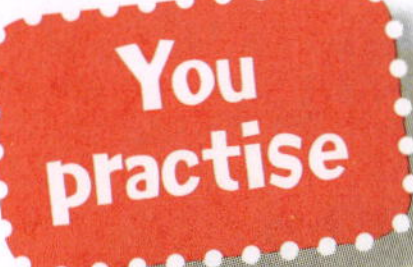

You practise Write the letter that matches the correct answer above to find a hidden message.

T	F	R	O	A	T	R	F	E	S
4c	3c	6c	20c	5c	9c	18c	10c	25c	24c

BOB time!

10% AND MORE

10% means 10 out of 100 or $\frac{1}{10}$.
Finding 10% is the same as finding $\frac{1}{10}$.

You already know that $\frac{1}{10}$ of $1 is 10c because you know there are ten 10c coins in $1. You can use this to help you find 10% of any whole number amount.

10% of $5

If 10% of $1 = 10c

Then 10% of $5 = 50c (5 × 10c)

30% of $1

If 10% of $1 is 10c

Then 30% is 3 times as much, which is 30c

11% of $1

If 10% of $1 = 10c and

1% of $1 = 1c

Then 11% of $1 is 11c (10c + 1c = 11c)

Remember that 10% of $1 is 10c. This fact will often come in handy.

We practise

Show how to find 10% of $8 using what you already know.

10% of $1 = 10c

10% of $8 = 80c

Show how to find 11% of $8 using what you already know.

10% of $8 = 80c

1% of $8 = 8c

11% of $8 = 88c

You practise Answer these percentage questions.

1 10% of $2 = ________ c

10% of $8 = ________ c

10% of $10 = $ ________

20% of $10 = $ ________

20% of $20 = $ ________

11% of $1 = ________ c

11% of $3 = ________ c

21% of $1 = ________ c

13% of $2 = ________ c

13% of $5 = ________ c

Remember that **10% of $1 is 10c** and **1% of $1 is 1c** to help you with these questions.

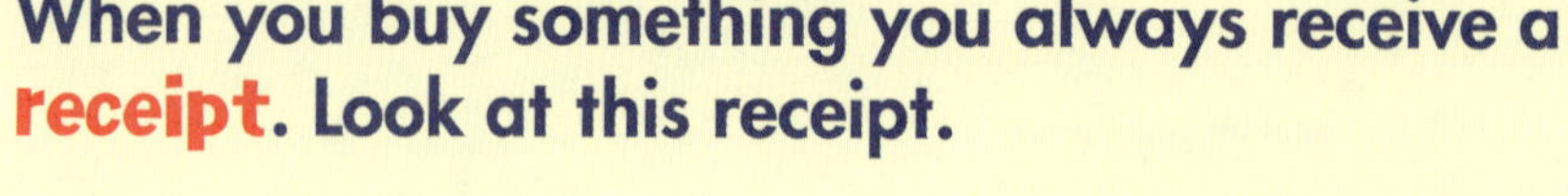

Unit 14: Shopping receipts and GST

All Australian shopping receipts have this information.

When you buy something you always receive a **receipt**. Look at this receipt.

Did you notice the 10% tax? In Australia there is a **goods and services tax (GST)** of **10%** on most items. The receipt shows the **actual amount** (cost price) as well as the **GST** that the shop must pay to the government.

We practise

How much GST should a shopkeeper charge for a pair of jeans at the cost price of $30?

10% of $1 is 10c

So 10% of $30 is 30 × 10c

GST = $3

Complete this shopping receipt.

Cap $12.00

GST $1.20

Total $13.20

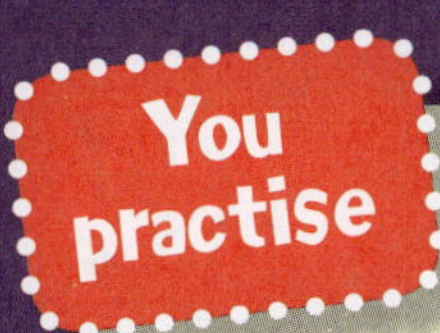

How much GST should a shopkeeper charge for each of these items?

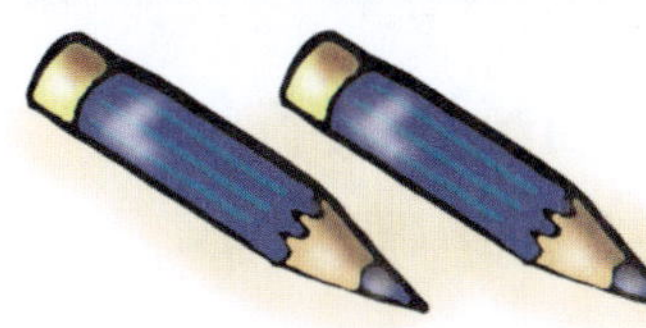

Pencils $10 GST = $ ________

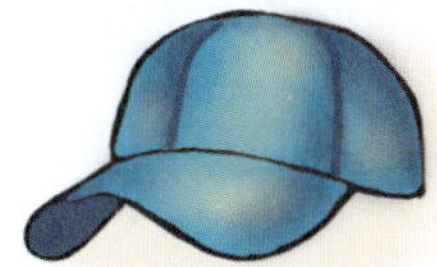

Cap $15 GST = $ ________

Book $18 GST = $ ________

You practise

Complete these receipts.

Pack of Cards $3

GST ________ c

Total $ ________

Remember GST is 10%.

T-shirt $30

GST $ ________

Total $ ________

Magazine $13

GST $ ________

Total $ ________

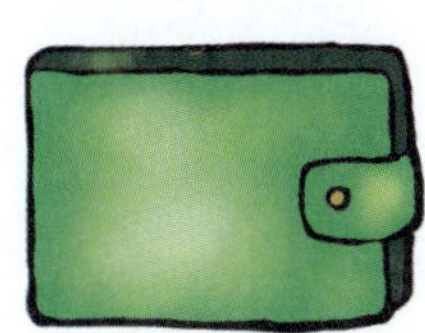

Wallet $32

GST $ ________

Total $ ________

BOB time!

50%, 25% AND 20%

There are some **useful percentages** that are easy to learn and to remember.

50% is an easy percentage to remember because it means 50 out of 100, which is $\frac{1}{2}$.

50% of \$40 is \$20 50% of \$100 is \$50

And if you know 50%, then it is not hard to find 25%, because 25% is half of 50%. Look at these steps.

25% of \$80

Step 1 Find 50% or half = \$40

Step 2 Halve it again to find 25% = \$20

Finding 20% is easy too.

20 out of 100 is the same as finding $\frac{1}{5}$.
Look at these steps.

20% of \$40

Step 1 Find 10% = \$4

Step 2 Double it to find 20% = \$8

To find 50% all you need to do is halve the price.

25 out of 100 is the same as $\frac{1}{4}$ of 100.

We practise

Show how to find 25% of \$60.

50% of \$60 = \$30

so 25% of \$60 = \$15

Show how to find 75% of \$12.

50% of \$12 = \$6

and 25% of \$12 = \$3

so 75% of \$12 = \$9

You practise

Answer these percentage questions.

1. 50% of \$50 = \$ ________

2. 25% of \$40 = \$ ________

3. 25% of \$1 = ________ c

4. 50% of \$110 = \$ ________

Finding 75% is the same as finding 50% + 25%. It's easy when you split percentages into parts that you know.

Show how to find the following percentages.

5. **25% of \$80**

50% of \$80 = \$ ________

so 25% of \$80 = \$ ________

7. **70% of \$1**

50% of \$1 = ________ c

and 20% of \$1 = ________ c

so 70% of \$1 = ________ c

6. **20% of \$80**

10% of \$80 = \$ ________

so 20% of \$80 = \$ ________

8. **75% of \$2**

50% of \$2 = \$ ________

and 25% of \$2 = ________ c

so 75% of \$2 = \$ ________

BOB time!

UNIT 16

ON SPECIAL

When there is a **sale** or a **special offer** you might see signs such as:

15% off storewide

10% off!

Save 30%

It is useful to know how to work out in your head what the **sale price** is and how much you will save.

Remember to split 20% into 10% + 10% to make it easier.

Look at this example.

Normally $35
TODAY ONLY
20% off

Here is how to work out the sale price.

Step 1 20% of $35 = $7 saving

Step 2 $35 – $7 = $28

Was $89.50
Now
50% off

Step 1 50% of $90 = $45 saving

Step 2 $90 – $45 = $45

We practise

Show how to find the sale price of a $25 item that has 10% off.

10% of $25 = $2.50 saving

Sale Price $25 – $2.50 = $22.50

Show how to find the sale price of a $40 item that has 15% off.

10% of $40 = $4

5% of $40 = $2

15% of $40 = $6 saving

Sale Price $40 – $6 = $34

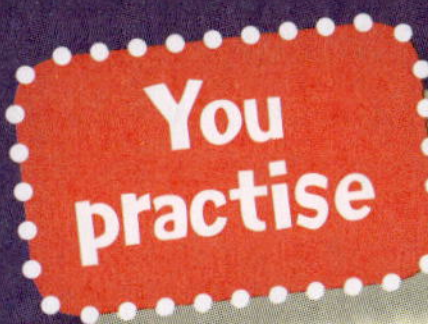

What is the sale price for these items?

1 **Shoes $80** 25% off

Saving $ ______

Sale price $ ______

Remember to split the percentages to make it easy to work out the savings.

2 **Tennis racquet $120** 25% off

Saving $ ______

Sale price $ ______

3 **Shorts $80** 35% off

Saving $ ______

Sale price $ ______

4 **Skipping rope $12** 15% off

Saving $ ______

Sale price $ ______

5 **Kite $100** 22% off

Saving $ ______

Sale price $ ______

6 **Bike $200** 35% off

Saving $ ______

Sale price $ ______

MAKING A BUDGET

Jake wants a new bicycle that costs $199.95.

Jake's dad is giving him 10% and his mum is giving him 15% for a deposit so that he can put it on layby. He also gets $5 a week pocket money and his parents are going to pay him for doing chores. Here is the list of chores.

Empty dishwasher	50c a day
Clean the car	$5 a fortnight
Vacuum the house	$2.50 a week
Mow the lawn	$5 a fortnight

Sounds hard, but it's easy if you make a step-by-step plan.

How long will it take Jake to save for the bicycle?
Look at these steps to help you work out the answer.

Step 1 Round up $199.95		$200
Step 2 How much does Jake have for the deposit?	10% of $200 (dad) = $20 15% of $200 (mum) = $30	$150 left to pay
Step 3 What is Jake's income for a **fortnight**?	Pocket money 2 × $5 = $10 Dishwasher 14 × 50c = $7 Cleaning car $5 Vacuuming 2 × $2.50 = $5 Mowing $5	$32 a fortnight or $16 a week
Step 4 How long will it take Jake to save $150?	$150 ÷ 32	**5 fortnights or 10 weeks**

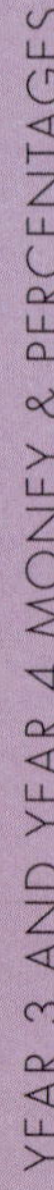

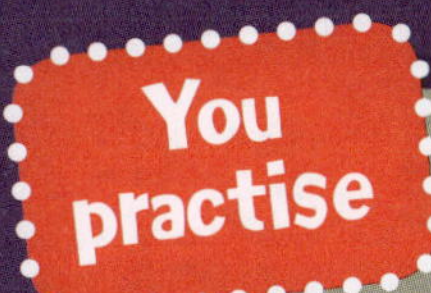

Work out how long it will take Clare and James to save for the things they want.

Clare wants to buy a scooter for $149.95. She has saved 20% deposit. She gets $10 a week for pocket money and $10 a week for doing chores.

Step 1 Round $149.95		$ ______
Step 2 How much does Clare have for the deposit?	20% of $ ______ = $ ______	$ ______ left to pay
Step 3 What is Clare's income for a week?	$ ______ + $ ______	$ ______ a week
Step 4 How long will it take Clare to save $ ______?	$ ______ ÷ ______ = ______	______ **weeks**

James wants to buy a scooter for $249.50 and has saved 30% deposit. He gets $10 a week for pocket money and $5 a week for doing the vacuuming.

Step 1 Round $249.50		$ ______
Step 2 How much does James have for the deposit?	30% of $ ______ = $ ______	$ ______ left to pay
Step 3 What is James' income for a week?	$ ______ + $ ______	$ ______ a week
Step 4 How long will it take James to save $ ______?	$ ______ ÷ ______ = ______	______ **weeks**

BOB time!

CALCULATOR PERCENTAGES

Some percentages are hard to work out in your head and it would be easier to use a calculator.

However, before you reach for your calculator, you can **estimate** the answer.

Look at this example.

Find $7\frac{1}{2}$% of \$36

Step 1 10% of \$36 = \$3.60

Step 2 Half of \$3.60 (5%) = \$1.80

Step 3 $7\frac{1}{2}$% is halfway between 5% and 10%, so the answer will be a little more than \$2

Now use the calculator. Here is the key sequence to use:

36 [×] 7·5 [%]

You will see the answer 2.7 in the display, which really means \$2.70.

You can't enter $\frac{1}{2}$ on the calculator so you have to use the decimal form, .5. Remember, don't press the [=] key!

We practise

Give a rough estimate for $9\frac{1}{2}$% of \$36 and then find the answer using your calculator.

Estimate 10% of \$36 = \$3.60

Key Sequence 36 [×] 9·5 [%]

Answer \$3.42

Give a rough estimate for $4\frac{1}{2}$% of \$45 and then find the answer using your calculator.

Estimate 5% of \$45 = \$2.25

Key Sequence 45 [×] 4·5 [%]

Answer \$2.03

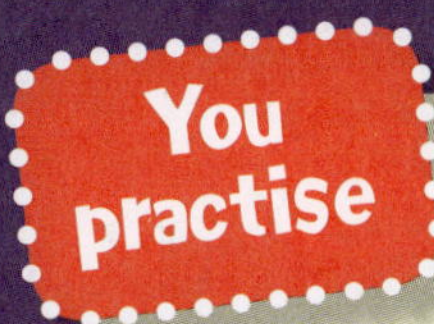

Give a rough estimate for each question and then find the answer using your calculator.

Use a calculator!

1 $7\frac{1}{2}$% of \$58

Estimate ______________

Key Sequence: ______________ ☐ ______________ ☐

Answer $ ______________

2 $8\frac{1}{2}$% of \$106

Estimate ______________

Key Sequence: ______________ ☐ ______________ ☐

Answer $ ______________

3 $3\frac{1}{2}$% of \$196

Estimate ______________

Key Sequence: ______________ ☐ ______________ ☐

Answer $ ______________

4 $2\frac{1}{2}$% of \$72

Estimate ______________

Key Sequence: ______________ ☐ ______________ ☐

Answer $ ______________

5 $6\frac{1}{2}$% of \$256

Estimate ______________

Key Sequence: ______________ ☐ ______________ ☐

Answer $ ______________

6 $22\frac{1}{2}$% of \$220

Estimate ______________

Key Sequence: ______________ ☐ ______________ ☐

Answer $ ______________

BOB time!

FOREIGN CURRENCIES

Each country has its own currency (coins and notes).
One thing that most currencies have in common is that they have a base unit, like our dollar, which is made up of 100 smaller units, like our cents.

This table shows some currencies from different countries.

Australia	China	UK	India
dollar	yuan	pound	rupee
100 cents	100 jiao	100 pence	100 paise

In Australia, to make $1.25 you use three coins ($1, 20c, 5c). In America, you only need two coins ($1 and a quarter).

This table shows some Australian and American coins.

Australia	USA
	penny (1 cent)
5 cents	nickel (5 cents)
10 cents	dime (10 cents)
20 cents	
	quarter (25 cents)
50 cents	half dollar (50 cents)
100 cents ($1)	dollar (100 cents)

We practise

If you have 200 paise, how many rupees do you have?

2 rupees

Using the least amount of American coins, how would you make $1·30?

dollar + quarter + nickel

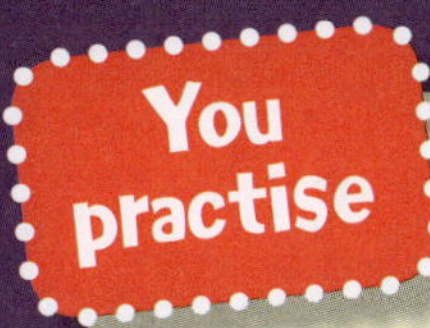

What is the equivalent amount in each currency?

300 jiao ______________ yuan

400 pence ______________ pounds

Use the table on the opposite page to help you work out these amounts.

500 paise ______________ rupees

4 2 quarters ______________ cents

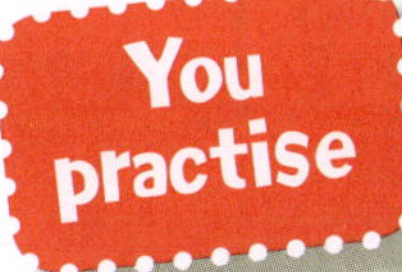

Show how to make these amounts using the least amount of American coins.

40 cents ________ + ________ + ________

75 cents ________ + ________

$1.40 ________ + ________ + ________ + ________

$2.60 ________ + ________ + ________

BOB time!

PROBLEM SOLVING

Clare and Jake are arguing over who has saved the most money.

"How much money have you saved?" Clare asks Jake.

"I have 25% of $80," he says. "What about you?"

"I have $17\frac{1}{2}$% of $100," she replies.

Who has saved the most money, Clare or Jake?

The important information is highlighted in blue and what has to be found out is highlighted in pink.

Remember to use the calculator to multiply the amount by the percentage, but **don't press the = key!**

Look at these steps to find an answer.

Step 1 How much Jake has saved?	25% of $80 is the same as finding a quarter of $80, which is $20.
Step 2 How much Clare has saved?	Use the calculator if you like, but finding a % of $100 is easy. $17\frac{1}{2}$% of $100 = $17.50
Step 3 Compare the two amounts.	$20 is more than $17.50
Step 4 Write your answer as a sentence.	Jake has saved the most money.

We practise

Aunty Jane sent $120 to be shared between her nephews and nieces. Jake, the oldest, gets 30% and Clare gets 25%. The twins, Jo and Trish, both get the same amount. How much does each child receive?

Step 1 How much does Jake get? $36

Step 2 How much does Clare get? $30

Step 3 How much is left for the twins to share? $54 = $27 each

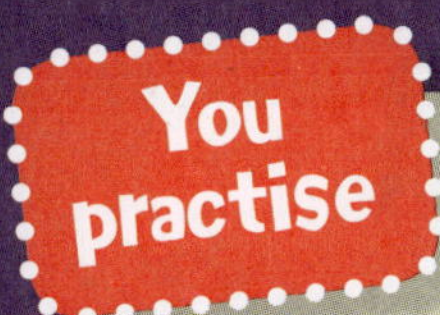

Highlight the important information and solve the problems.

1 Jake has $20 to spend on a picnic for three people. Cakes cost $1.75 each, sandwiches $2.20 each and drinks $1.45 each. He wants to buy one of each item for each person. How much will it cost him? $ ________
How much change will he receive? $ ________

2 Clare has paid 45% towards her $199.50 game console. Her mum is paying the rest. How much does mum have to pay? $ ________

3 "How did you go at the Spellathon?" Mum asked Jake. She is paying 10c for every one of the 40 words that Jake spelt correctly. Jake said he got 15% of them wrong. How much will Jake's mum have to pay? $ ________

4 Fill in the missing information on this receipt.

WILO Superstore

21.1.2012

Bread	$2
Cheese	$6.50
Subtotal	$________
GST	$________
Total	$________

Remember to use your calculator for any tricky percentages, but make an estimate first.

5 "$17\frac{1}{2}$% off HD TVs this week" the advertisement says. How much does a $748 HD TV cost this week? $ ________

6 T-shirts are $25 each, but if you buy four there is 30% off the price. How much do four T-shirts cost? $ ________ How much does each one cost? $ ________

7 Jake has a collection of American coins: 10 dimes, 3 nickels, 5 quarters and 6 half dollars. What is the value in American dollars of Jake's collection?
$ ________

8 Clare has 5 American coins that together are worth $2.30.
What coins does she have? ______________________________

BOB time!

TEST 1

 What is the value of these coins? ________     

 Write a speed counting sequence for these coins.     

___ ___ ___ ___ ___

 Which coins would you use to pay for this apple using the least number of coins?

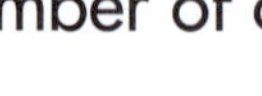

 $1.65 $ ________ + ________c + ________c + ________c

 Round these amounts to the nearest dollar.

$1.85 ________ 75c ________ $1.20 ________

 How much to buy these two items?

$1.35 + 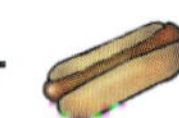 $1.75 Total = $ ________

 Show how to round up or down to estimate how much for these three items.

$1.75 + $2.15 + $41.65 $ ________ + $ ________ + $ ________ = $ ________

 Show on a number line how much change from $10 after spending $5.15.

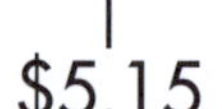

$5.15 $10 Change: $ ________

 Show how to round and adjust to work out how much for four drinks at $1.95 each.

Round: $1.95 ________ to $ ________ 4 × $ ________ = $ ________

Adjust: 4 × ________c = ________c $ ________ +/− ________c = $ ________

 Show how to split 75c to make it easy to work out what six oranges at 75c each cost.

75c = ________c + ________c

6 × ________ = $ ________

6 × ________ = $ ________ Total $ ________

TEST 2

1 What change should I get from $10 for a lunchbox that costs $6.50? Show your answer on the number line.

$6.50 $10

2 How much for three muffins at $1.95 each and three apples at 75 cents each?

× 3 × 3 $ ______

3 What is 10% of $55? $ ______

4 What is 1% of $65? ______ c

5 What is 11% of $40? $ ______

6 Complete this shopping docket.

MyLO Superstore

27.1.2012

Laundry detergent	$6.60
GST	$______
Total	$______

7 What is 25% of $40? Saving $ ______ Sale price $ ______

8 What is 75% of $80? Saving $ ______ Sale price $ ______

9 How much for a $40 T-shirt that has a 20% discount?

Saving $ ______ Sale price $ ______

10 Show the calculator key sequence and answer for $17\frac{1}{2}$% of $60.

Estimate ______

Key Sequence: ______ ☐ ______ ☐

Answer $ ______

ANSWERS

Unit 1

1 10 20 30 40 50 60 70 = 70c
2 5 10 15 20 25 30 35 40 45 50 = 50c
3 20 40 60 80 100 = 100c or $1
4 50 100 150 = 150c or $1.50
5 5c 5c 5c 5c 5c 5c 5c
6 10c 10c 10c 10c 10c 10c
7 20c 20c 20c 20c
8 50c 50c 50c 50c 50c

Unit 2

1 50 60 70 80 85 = 85c
2 20 40 50 55 60 = 60c
3 50 70 80 90 100 105 110 = 110c or $1.10
4 40c
5 75c
6 $1.05

Unit 3

1 $3 + 65c = $3.65
2 $4 + 80c = $ 4.80
3 $2 + 135c = $3.35
4 $4 + 110c = $ 5.10

5 

6 

7 

8 

Unit 4

1 $1 + $1 = $2
50c + 50c = 100c
5c + 5c = 10c Total $3.10

2 $1 + $1 = $2
20c + 20c = 40c
10c + 10c = 20c
5c + 5c = 10c Total $2.70

3 $1 + $1 = $2
20c + 20c = 40c Total $2.40

4 $2 + $1 = $3
20c + 20c = 40c
5c = 5c Total $3.45

5 $1 + $1 + $1 = $3
50c + 50c + 30c = 130c
5c + 5c + 5c = 15c Total $4.45

6 $2 + $1 = $3
20c + 20c = 40c
5c + 5c = 10c
10c = 10c Total $3.60

Unit 5

1 Change = 65c

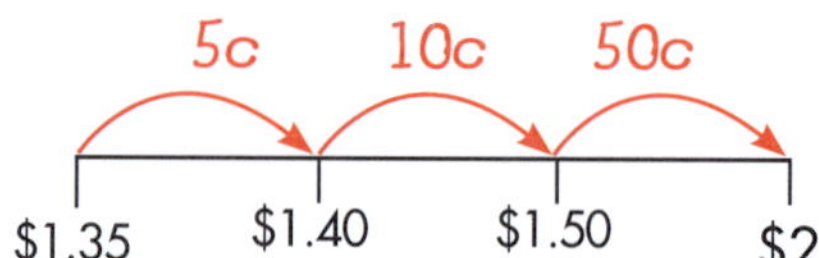

2 Change = $1.75

3 Change = $1.50

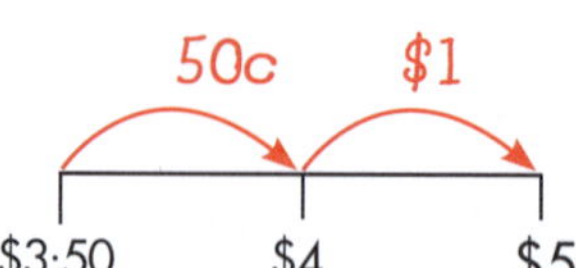

4 Change = $7.30

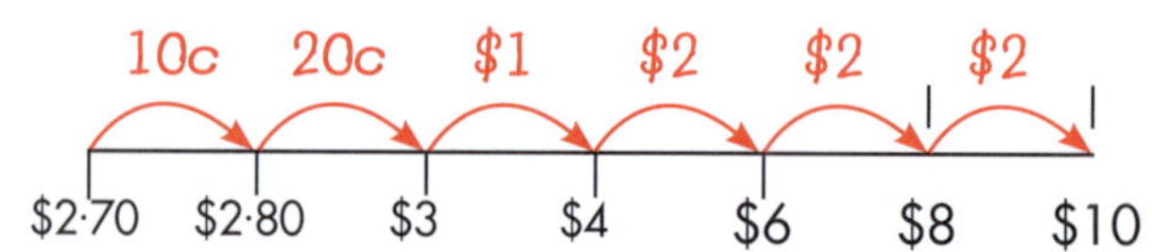

5 Change = $12.50

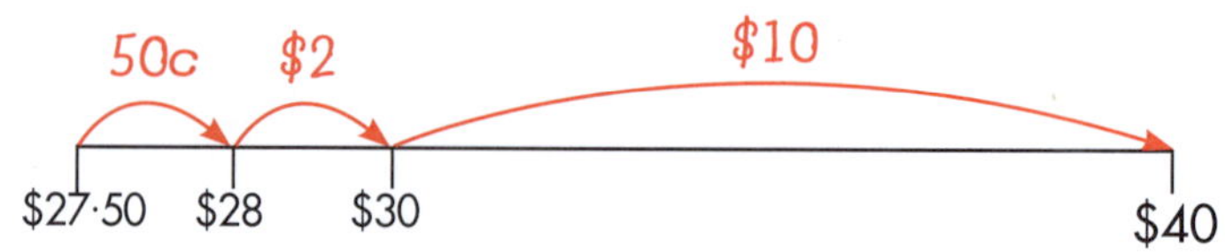

ANSWERS

Unit 6

1 $2.01 rounds down to $2 Y
2 $1.52 rounds down to $1.50 O
3 $2.32 rounds down to $2.30 U
4 $8.98 rounds up to $9 D
5 $2.36 rounds to down to $2.35 I
6 $7.02 rounds down to $7 D
7 $5.56 rounds down to $5.55 W
8 $3.38 rounds up to $3.40 E
9 $6.56 rounds down to $6.55 L
10 $1.68 rounds up to $1.70 L

Unit 7

1 $2.20 rounds down to $2
$2.95 rounds up to $3
Estimated amount $5
2 $3.85 rounds up to $4
$3.90 rounds up to $4
Estimated amount $8
3 $6.80 rounds up to $7
$4.25 rounds down to $4
Estimated amount $11
4 $1.50
$7.50
Estimate $9 Actual $8.80
5 $3
$4
$4
Estimate $11 Actual $10.49
6 $1
$3.50
$3
Estimate $7.50 Actual $7.40

Unit 8

1 Round: $1.45 up to $1.50
4 × $1.50 = $6
Adjust: 4 × 5c = 20c
$6 – 20c = $5.80
2 Round: 95c up to $1
3 × $1 = $3
Adjust: 3 × 5c = 15c
$3 – 15c = $2.85
3 Round: $1.90 up to $2
6 × $2 = $12
Adjust: 6 × 10c = 60c
$12 – 60c = $11.40
4 $2.50 = $2 + 50c
4 × $2 = $8
4 × 50c = $2
Total = $10
5 $2.55 = $2 + 50c + 5c
3 × $2 = $6
3 × 50c = $1.50
3 × 5c = 15c
Total = $7.65
6 75c = 50c + 20c + 5c
5 × 50c = $2.50
5 × 20c = $1
5 × 5 = 25c
Total: $3.75

Unit 9

1	$1.45	99c	$1.95	$3.75	$3.25
2	$2.90	$1.98	$3.90	$7.50	$6.50
3	$4.35	$2.97	$5.85	$11.25	$9.75
4	$5.80	$3.96	$7.80	$15.00	$13.00
5	$7.25	$4.95	$9.75	$18.75	$16.25
6	$8.70	$5.94	$11.70	$22.50	$19.50
7	$10.15	$6.93	$13.65	$26.25	$22.75
8	$11.60	$7.92	$15.60	$30.00	$26.00

Unit 10

1 5c
2 Two $2 and one 20c
3 $1.50 + $2 + $1 + $2.50 + $3 = $10
4 $5.55
5 Yes
6 A drink and an apple
7 $15.30
8 An apple, a drink and a muffin or a burger, a drink and a banana
9 $8.45 5c, 20c, 20c, $2, $2, $2, $2
10 6 × $1.85 = $11.10

ANSWERS

Unit 11

Answers will vary.

Unit 12

Find each percentage amount and use it to find the hidden message.

1	24c	S
2	4c	T
3	5c	A
4	6c	R
5	25c	E
6	10c	F
7	3c	F
8	20c	O
9	18c	R
10	9c	T

Unit 13

1. 20c
2. 80c
3. $1
4. $2
5. $4
6. 11c
7. 33c
8. 21c
9. 26c
10. 65c

Unit 14

1	$1	
2	$1.50	
3	$1.80	
4	GST	30c
	Total	$3.30
5	GST	$3
	Total	$33
6	GST	$1.30
	Total	$14.30
7	GST	$3.20
	Total	$35.20

Unit 15

1. $25
2. $10
3. 25c
4. $55
5. 50% of $80 = $40, so 25% of $80 = $20
6. 10% of $80 = $8, so 20% of $80 = $16
7. 50% of $1 = 50c and 20% of $1 = 20c, so 70% of $1 = 70c
8. 50% of $2 = $1 and 25% of $2 = 50c, so 75% of $2 = $1.50

Unit 16

1	Saving	$20
	Sale price	$60
2	Saving	$30
	Sale price	$90
3	Saving	$28
	Sale price	$52
4	Saving	$1.80
	Sale price	$10.20
5	Saving	$22
	Sale price	$78
6	Saving	$70
	Sale price	$130

Unit 17

Step 1 Round $149.95		$150
Step 2 How much does Clare have for the deposit?	20% of $150 = $30	$120 left to pay
Step 3 What is Clare's income for a week?	$10 + $10	$20 a week
Step 4 How long will it take Clare to save $120?	$120 ÷ 20 = 6	6 weeks

Step 1 Round $249.50		$250
Step 2 How much does James have for the deposit?	30% of $250 = $75	$175 left to pay
Step 3 What is James' income for a week?	$10 + $5	$15 a week
Step 4 How long will it take James to save $175?	$175 ÷15	12 weeks

ANSWERS

Unit 18

1 Estimate $4
Key Sequence 58 × 7.5%
Answer $4.35

2 Estimate $9
Key Sequence 106 × 8.5%
Answer $9.01

3 Estimate $6.50
Key Sequence 196 × 3.5%
Answer $6.86

4 Estimate $2
Key Sequence 72 × 2.5%
Answer $1.80

5 Estimate $15
Key Sequence 256 × 6.5%
Answer $16.64

6 Estimate $50
Key Sequence 220 × 22.5%
Answer $49.50

Unit 19

1 3 yuan
2 4 pounds
3 5 rupees
4 50 cents
5 quarter + dime + nickel
6 half dollar + quarter
7 dollar + quarter + dime + nickel
8 two dollars + half dollar + dime

Unit 20

1 $16.20; $3.80
2 $109.75
3 $3.40
4 Subtotal $8.50
GST 85c
Total $9.35
5 $617.10
6 $70; $17.50
7 $5.40
8 One dollar, two half dollars, one quarter and a nickel
Or
Two dollars and three dimes

Test 1

1 $1.20
2 50c + 20c + 10c + 10c + 5c
3 $1 + 50 + 10c + 5c
4 $2 $1 $1
5 $3.10
6 $2 + $2 + $42 = $46
7 $4.85

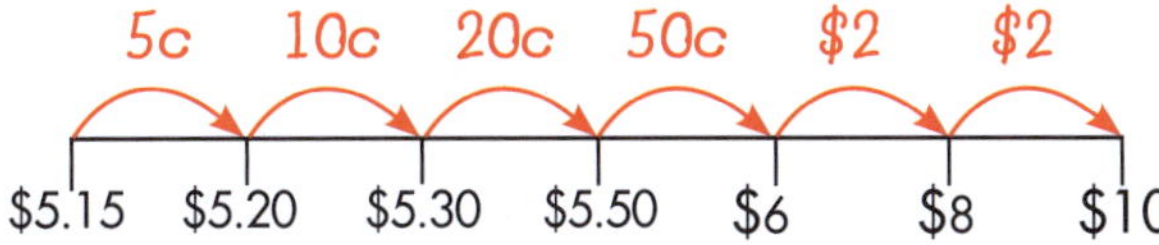

8 Round $1.95 to $2
4 × $2 = $8
Adjust 4 × 5c = 20c
$8 – 20c = $7.80

9 50c + 25c = 75c
6 × 50c = $3
6 × 25c = $1.50
Total = $4.50

Test 2

1 $3.50

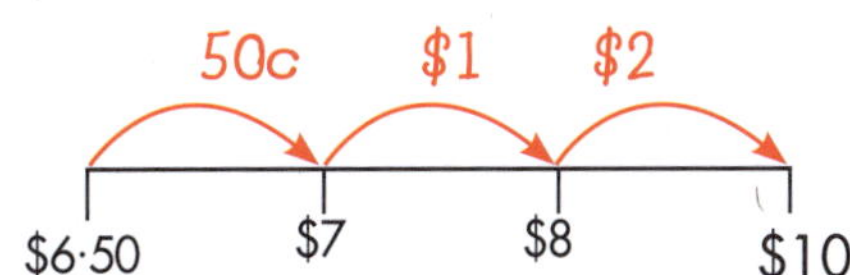

2 $8.10
3 $5.50
4 65c
5 $4.40
6 GST 66c
Total $7.26
7 $10 $30
8 $60 $20
9 $8 $32
10 $10
60 × 17.5%
$10.50

Back to Basics Money & Percentages Year 3 and Year 4

Reprinted 2016, 2018, 2023

ISBN: 978 1 74215 937 9

Published by Pascal Press
PO Box 250
Glebe NSW 2037
www.pascalpress.com.au
contact@pascalpress.com.au

Author: Ann Baker
Publisher: Lynn Dickinson
Editor: Eliza Hope
Proofreader: Tim Learner
Design and illustration: Janice Bowles
Page layout and technical illustration: Louise Rhodes
Printed by Wai Man Book Binding (China) Ltd.